May 11, 2003
Mother's Day

Mothers & Daughters

MADELEINE L'ENGLE

Photography by **MARIA ROONEY**

Gramercy Books · New York

This 2001 edition is published by Gramercy Books™, an imprint of Random House Value Publishing, Inc., 280 Park Avenue, New York, NY 10017, by arrangement with Harold Shaw Publishers, Waterbrook Press, a division of Random House, Inc.

Gramercy Books™ and design are trademarks of Random House Value Publishing, Inc.

Printed and bound in Singapore.

Random House
New York · Toronto · London · Sydney · Auckland
http://www.randomhouse.com/

Library of Congress Cataloging-in-Publication Data

L'Engle, Madeleine.
    Mothers & daughters / Madeleine L'Engle ; photography by Maria Rooney.
        p. cm.
    Originally published: Wheaton, Ill. : Harold Shaw Publishers, 1997.
    ISBN 0-517-21961-1
    1. Mothers and daughters. 2. Mothers and daughters--Pictorial works. I. Title: Mothers and daughters. II. Rooney, Maria. III. Title.

HQ755.85 .L45 2001
306.874'3--dc21
                                                    2001033067

9 8 7 6 5 4 3 2 1

Contents

Acknowledgments

During my search for many different kinds of mothers and daughters for this book, I have been greatly enriched by their diverse stories of courage and love. There are all ages of mothers and daughters here, connected biologically and by adoption. Together we have delighted in exploring the many phases we go through: tender young mothers with their babies, moms with toddlers and tomboys, moms with impatient teenagers, mothers with their adult daughters, and women who are both mothers and daughters.

Collaborating with my mother on this book has been a revelation to me. We have both learned a lot, we have been creative together, and, most important, we have gained a deeper understanding of each other and the unique love that ties mothers and daughters together.

Maria Rooney

A Mother's Love

Introduction

Maria Rooney

A mother's love is awesome. It is something I do not take for granted.

My father died when I was six years old, and my mother died a year later. Madeleine L'Engle, my soon-to-be new mother, brought me from New York City to their home in the country. My new family was familiar to me because we had spent many happy times together, and I had even had all of my birthdays at their house. But I was seven years old, an only child, and completely shell-shocked when I was suddenly thrust into this family, with two children already there. All of our lives changed.

My new mother, also shocked by the untimely death of her dear friend, suddenly found herself a mother of three children instead of two. Thus, ours has been a stormy relationship. We had to learn to be mother and daughter, and the learning started immediately. The learning continues, and the love continues to grow between this mother and daughter. And that is why I am in awe of the power of a mother's love, and also why I cannot take it for granted.

Look at you!
Ten fingers and ten toes!
Two eyes and one nose!
One mouth and no teeth!
A belly button that was once part of me
and now you're wholly you—
a gift from God and the holy angels
and, my husband might add,
he had a small part in it, too.
Thank you, God, for this gift,
and all that brought it to be.
Help me to treasure this child
as your child, to love as you love.
Help me to rejoice in her always.

I said to my baby,
"You're here! My baby is here! God's gift is here!"
Oh, God, bless me and my baby,
bless me and my husband,
and if you give us other children,
bless them too.
Bless our family.
Help us to be like your family,
the one, holy, and indivisible Trinity.
Help us to love each other with your love. Amen

God, you made great galaxies and clouds of flaming gas and burning suns. Surely they are no more exciting to you than one small child laughing with love.

O Holy One,
how precious are your creatures to you
who made us all.
When I check my child at night
and see that lovely, sleeping face, some of your
love flows over and through me
and you show me how to love.
O Lord, help me to remember when she's awake.

Lord, help me to be a mother,
a mother who is kind and gentle,
a mother who is firm and strong,
a mother who loves to say yes,
but who loves enough to say no.
Let my trust in you permeate
every moment of my life,
so my daughter may see and feel
and live in that trust. So it is her trust, too.

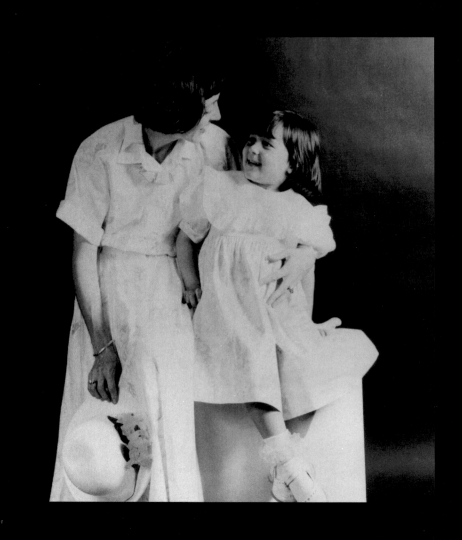

It would be wonderful, O Holy One,
if we mothers and daughters were always perfect:

"If I never raised my voice in annoyance—"
"If I never snapped back."
"If I didn't have to remind you at least twice a day—"
"If I could remember to hang up my clothes."
"If I realized, all the time, how precious you are to me—"
"If I never forgot you're a pretty good mother, most of the time."

But we're not perfect.
Just a human mother and daughter.
Help us to make the best of us, Lord.

Daughter, darling,
I love you.
I know I don't always understand.
My mother didn't always understand me.
That's the way it is with mothers and daughters.
But I love you. I will always love you.

My daughter is my delight. I laugh with joy. Surely
Mary must have delighted in Jesus. Surely Mary's
mother must have laughed with her. All the way
back to Eve mothers have laughed with delight.
Who laughed with Eve?

What are you thinking, O my little one?
You are looking far away at something I cannot see.
You have your thoughts and I have mine.
You are you and I am me.
You are my daughter and I am your mother.
And that is forever.

When I was little I wore my mother's hat, too.
Is that the way we play at growing up?
At wondering what it will be like to be a mother?
In our lives, how many hats will we wear?

Oh, Mom, I'm okay, aren't I?
You laugh when I tell silly stories.
If my feelings are hurt, you hug me and tell me I'm wonderful.
If I do something I shouldn't do, you get cross but you still love me.
Mom, you're okay, too.

Mom, we have such fun!
Does God have fun when we have fun?
Does God like to play?
I think that when we laugh together God laughs, too.

It's all right, isn't it?
You hold me and I'm safe.
Outside I hear the noises of the street.
Shouting and sirens and even gunshots.
But you hold me and tell me it's God's world.
And it's all right.

Mothers & Daughters

Introduction

Madeleine L'Engle

We all begin our lives as daughters, we women, and many of us end up as mothers, too, balancing the double role.

I was not a little girl who played with dolls, perhaps because I was an only child in an apartment in a large city, and solitary. Perhaps because my parents traveled a great deal, and I saw less of my mother than most children did, I had no role model for playing mother to my dolls. So my own family was all the more important to me.

I did play with paper dolls, but these I drew and colored myself, designing elaborate wardrobes and making up stories about them. From this one might think I'd become a fashion designer, but I was more interested in story than in fashion.

I came late in my parents' lives which had settled into a pattern which had little place for a child, though I was a much wanted child. But I didn't see a great deal of my parents, even when they were not traveling. This was especially true in the evenings, because my father was a music and drama critic, and they were out at the theatre, opera, concerts. I loved my parents. I thought they were perfect, and perhaps their human imperfections would have been more apparent to me if I'd been with them more. But not only did I think they were perfect, I knew that they were people of complete integrity. In the old-fashioned sense of the words, which has nothing to do with money or social position, my mother was a lady and my father was a gentleman. They taught me courtesy, though too often my manners were hidden by shyness.

Much of my mother's attention went to my father, because he had been gassed in the trenches in the First World War and was never well after that. The sound of his painful coughing is part of my childhood. It took him until I was seventeen to finish coughing his lungs out. I could never forget war and what it did to people, and I am passionately pacifistic, yet I have lived in a century of war.

The greatest gift my mother gave me, besides her love, was story. She was a wonderful storyteller, especially about her childhood in the South. All her friends were cousins. At each corner of St. John's Episcopal Church lived one of her great-uncles. Many of the families were large, and so the generations were mixed. One of her cousins had the pleasure of dandling his baby great-aunt over his shoulder.

My mother's childhood was spent in the aftermath of the War between the States, and nobody had any money—nobody except the carpetbaggers and others who took advantage of the ravaged South. But storytelling didn't cost anything, nor playing in the jungly areas around the town, where huge vines could be used as swings. The older young people enjoyed dancing and swimming in the great St. John's River. There was always plenty to do. My mother loved spending the night with either set of grandparents, and they, too, were full of stories.

Much more was demanded of Episcopalians in those days than when I was growing up. There was daily morning and evening prayer. My mother and her cousins knew the Bible well, the begats as well as the stories. On Sundays the only game they were allowed to play was the Bible Game, and that became part of my childhood, although it's better if played with a group.

Lent was kept seriously, which was a real deprivation because that was when the great theatre companies came south, and Episcopalians were not allowed to go to the theatre during Lent. Fasting wasn't difficult, because there wasn't much to eat at the best of times. A real treat was a spoonful of syrupy brown sugar from the big barrel in the pantry.

I was fascinated. "Tell me a story," I would beg, and my mother would take me in imagination back to her world so different from mine.

Her own household, despite three younger brothers, was quiet, polite, formal, and prudish. She was told nothing about the changes that come to a young girl's body, so they all came as frightening surprises. She was determined that this not happen to me, so when I was nine or ten I was given a book about procreation. What I remember are the photographs: pictures of a cherry tree in blossom; a pig surrounded by piglets; and finally, a human embryo. Explanations were simple and clear. And my mother was willing to answer any of my questions, which can't have been easy for her, so I am grateful for that, as for so much else. I have written about my mother at length in *The Summer of the Great-Grandmother,* a labor of love.

When it came my turn to be a mother, it was shortly after the end of the Second World War and things had changed again, and I had firm ideas of what I wanted my family to be like. I had had two books published, and I knew I needed to keep on writing, but I also wanted to bring up my own children, and even if we had been able to afford nannies, I wanted my children to know their mother and learn about life and love from me. My husband, Hugh, and I had hoped to have half a dozen children but, alas, after my son, my second child, was born, having more children was out of the question. But God has amazing ways of dealing with the impossible, and through the death of two close friends, our daughter Maria came to us. She was no stranger; she had spent all seven of her birthdays with us at Crosswicks; she was already family, but suddenly she was family in a different way, a shell-shocked child who had been betrayed by her universe. How do two loving but inexperienced parents bring security back to a small child? We believed that God had sent her to us as a special gift and a special responsibility. We tried to keep a regular, loving routine. Prayer time in the evening was the most important time of the day, the time when we could talk freely about God's love. How do you love a God who, it seems, has taken away your parents? The only way we felt we could help was to be as loving as possible ourselves, and as consistent. You can afford a little inconsistency with a secure child, but not with one whose universe has been smashed.

Ours has been a stormy relationship, with lots of misunderstandings on both sides, but it has also been undergirded by love, and that is what has made it creative and delightful as well as difficult. Would I want it to have been easy? Of course. But as I used to tell my children, things that are easy aren't worth much.

So, I have two daughters, totally different, totally dear. Josephine, my first babe, had her own traumas. The obstetrician after her birth left in half my placenta, and one day when she was three and a half weeks old, just as she was due to nurse, I had a violent hemorrhage, was rushed to the hospital with childbed fever, and nearly died. She didn't see me again for a month, and this radical and unexpected abandonment and separation was certainly a cause for insecurity.

But perhaps because we have been aware of the precariousness of all life, we have also treasured our relationships. I am very blessed in my daughters.

We're so alike.
And so different.
    When you do something I don't understand
I say, "How like your father."
        I say, "I'm not like anybody. I'm like me."
They say, "She has her Aunt Joy's brown eyes."
"And her Uncle Joe's quick temper."
"What about Aunt Matilda's always being quick to blame?"
I think I see that tendency—
        I say, "My daughter is who she is,
beautiful and unique. Creative and volatile.
Just as she is. I wouldn't change a thing."
        We are who we are, dear Lord.
I hope you wouldn't change us either.

There is something special and unique in the relationship between a mother and a daughter. We live within our mothers for nine months, are given birth (and that is a wild and violent experience for both mother and child), and for the first months and even years our mothers are little more than extensions of ourselves. We usually discover our mothers as separate people somewhere in adolescence, sometimes with startled pleasure, sometimes with indignation or resentment: How dare this person who has been in the world solely for my benefit become someone separate from me, a person in her own right?

It's hello and good-bye.
O, my darling girl, it's hard to let you go.
Be happy, be faithful, be loving.
When you remember that God is always with you,
remember that you are always in your mother's heart.

It is good to have special times to remember, bringing us close again as a family, even if geography sometimes separates us, and then we have to count on the phone to keep us together.

The birthday trees have always been a special pleasure in our family. We have trees of varying sizes in our little orchard because we replace the old trees when they go. For summer birthdays, we tie balloons and colorfully wrapped presents onto the lower branches, where little hands can reach them. A great pleasure for Maria and me was when we dressed the birthday trees for her son, Alexander, on his second birthday. We probably had more pleasure out of this than the baby, because the decorated trees reminded us of many other joyous occasions, while for Alexander a yellow balloon was the treasure of the day. He wasn't even particularly interested in opening his presents, despite the urgings of sibling and cousins. He wanted his yellow balloon, so we untied it, and he ran around with it, shrieking with joy.

Every once in a while at applesauce time I will be wandering through the orchard and will see the remnant of colored ribbon around the trunk of a tree and will cut it off to stop it from tightening against the tree, and I will remember.

A Daughter Grows Up

Introduction

Madeleine L'Engle

It happens.

It happens suddenly, when you aren't expecting it.

I had always resolved that I would never tell my daughters that they were too old to sit on my lap. Lap sitting hadn't quite ended when my eldest daughter, at the end of her sixth-grade year, was invited to a dance at the regional school where she would be going for junior high.

She was still a little girl. Her braids were gone because her younger sister on a dare one morning had cut one off. But she was still a little girl, with straight blonde hair and big, innocent eyes. We began talking about what she would wear to the dance. What were the other girls going to wear?

Her younger sister said, "Not a party dress. Kids don't wear party dresses anymore."

What do you wear to your first dance when you are finishing sixth grade? The children—yes, they were still children—would be driven to the regional school by various parents. It wouldn't be a dance where there were dates. But these children had gone through school together; they knew each other. At the dance there would be boys and girls from two other schools, who would be strangers to them. Who might be more grown up. Who would surely be different.

"Stockings!" our younger daughter exclaimed. "You have to have nylons!"

I didn't have many nylons myself. We lived in a dairy farm village, and I usually wore knee socks and comfortable moccasins. I dug through my drawer for a pair of nylons. My older daughter was only ten. My nylons were much too big for her. They sagged. We tried to pull them up, and it wasn't working.

"Where's Daddy?" our younger daughter asked.

Daddy had gone into town and brought back a pair of nylons the right size. After several phone calls for consultations with friends, we decided on a navy blue skirt and a pretty white blouse.

It's too soon, I thought. It's much too soon.

By the time our younger daughter was finishing sixth grade, we had left our little village and were back in New York, in Manhattan. The school dances were in the school, within easy walking distance. We could get a pair of nylons in a shop just around the corner and across the street. It was still too soon.

The dances were just a hint of what was to come, the dances where there were dates, the shopping for more grown-up clothes. The dinner table conversations were stretching us all.

The girls could hold their own, had their own opinions, no matter what the topic.

But I knew they were still children, at least the younger one, when, at dinner, she said, "Mother and Daddy, you're over the hill," and could not understand our laughter.

God, you honored touch
when you came to us as Jesus.
You took children on your lap
and let them put their little arms
around you.
How wonderful and sweet
is human touch.

Dear Mom,
I'm sorry.
I yelled at you.
I knew you were right, and I still yelled at you.
I wish you hadn't been right, but you were.
But even if you'd been wrong, I'm still sorry.
Forgive me?
Okay. Thank you.
Thank you, too, God, for helping me know
how sorry I am.

I like the way you kiss Daddy when he comes home
from work, like you really mean it, and you like it when
he kisses you, too.
I like the way you ask God to keep us and guard us.
I like the way you love God.
And me.

Dear God,
I'm glad I got born into a family that loves me.
My parents love each other and they love me.
I heard my friend's parents yell at each other.
And nobody said, "I'm sorry."
The parents of a boy I like are getting divorced.
There are three kids who live in a house that's falling
down and the yard is full of junk.
The family next door seems okay, except they never
sit down to eat together.
Dear God, sometimes I forget to say thank you for all
that you have given me.

Sometimes I think I would be better off without a mother to boss me around. She always thinks she knows best. She can thread a needle in two seconds. She can cook without burning all the pots and pans. She irons blouses so they look new. She tells me to make my bed so it doesn't look as though I'm still sleeping in it. She tells me not to hang my clothes on the floor. She tells me I had three fillings when I went to the dentist because I forget to brush my teeth, and because I eat too much junk food.

She nags.

What would I do if I didn't have her?

Help!

Thank you for my mother, God.

Thank you, God, for my mother and the family that
you have given me. Help me to care about those who
don't have all that I have, and help me to know how to
help others. I will try to do what you ask me to do.
I don't know how to help, but you will know.
Thank you.

My mother said to me,
"God made you just as you are, and that is the way God loves you. God wants you to be the most completely you, you can possibly be. God doesn't want you to be glamorous Shirley down the street or brilliant Paula in the grade above you. God wants you to be you, and that is how God loves you, as you."

I didn't believe my mother. I thought God wanted me to be prettier and smarter and different than I am.

But my mother kept on telling me, "I wouldn't want you to be one bit different from the way you are. It's you I love. And that's who God loves, too."

Sometimes when she tiptoes into my room long after I'm supposed to be asleep, and tucks the covers around me gently, and kisses me, softly, softly, then I know she's right.

I know, Mother.
I know my sister and I fight all the time.
She borrows my clothes and if she washes my shirts she doesn't iron them.
She keeps her share of the room a mess.
But what I know, even when I get maddest, is
if someone else criticizes me
or tries to hurt me,
she's there for me.
And I'm there for her.
Thanks.

We had a fight, my mother and I.
And then she said, "I love you."
And I cried.

"Be good," my mother says, instead of just good-bye.
"Be good. Be sweet. Be-have."
And I know she wants to go with me
to make sure I *do* behave.
But she can't. Not anymore.
I'm not a little girl, not now,
and that makes everything different.
But, Mom, I'll try.

When my mother dances
I forget that she's my mother.
She's a glamorous star
and her focus is on her dancing
and not on me. Until we stop.
And then she's my mother again.

When we dance together
is it like the stars dancing in the galaxies?
The galaxies in their swirling tango?
When we dance together
are we part of God's original ballet?

I said to my mother,
"It's not fair.
I have more jobs than she does.
You let her get away with all kinds of stuff
and you make me do her share.
You let her do all kinds of things you don't let me do.
You dump it all on me. . . .
What? You'll let us change jobs?
Really? Terrific! . . .
Yes, of course I'll think it over. . . .
Okay, okay.
I'll just keep my old jobs."

"Who do you love most?"

"I love both of you most."

"You can't love both of us most.
You have to love one of us more than the other."

"Okay, I love one of you more than the other."

"Which one, then?"

"Both of you?"

"I think you love her more than you love me."

"My sweetie, isn't this rather silly?
Is what you want for me to say that I love you most?"

"No! I want you to say that you love both of us most!"

"That's what I say!"

"Okay!"

Mother,
we have fun together.
When it rains and we put a puzzle all over the table and put it back together, that's fun.

We have fun when my friend comes over and you let us make cookies and then help us clean up. And eat them, too.

I like the way there's always room for one more at dinner.
I like the way you laugh, like little bells.
I like the way you let me be me.
I like the way you let God let you be you, too.

My friend's mother died.
She was sick a long time.
We got used to her being sick.
But not dead.
I know we will all die.
I don't understand.
    My mother says nobody understands
and that's why we need faith,
faith that because Jesus died
and rose from the dead
we no longer need to fear death.
I am afraid. I am afraid for my friend
because she has no mother to come home to.
My mother puts her arms around me and we cry.
My mother says death is like birth
and that my friend's mother is still alive.
    "I believe that with all my soul,"
my mother says, "but that doesn't stop us from hurting now.
Jesus hurt, too, and in his love, his love given in our love,
all our hurts will heal."

I said to my mother, "You don't understand. It was different when you were my age. Kids didn't think the way we do now. You don't get it."

I said to my friend, "You don't understand. How could you let me down this way? How could you do without me?"

I said to God, "You don't understand. You're mean."

I went to bed. I stuck my head under the covers and wouldn't say good night to anyone.

I woke up in the middle of the night. My covers had all been straightened out. My old bear had been put on the pillow beside me. Like a kiss. My mother's kiss.

God's kiss.

A teenager says, "My mother has forgotten what it was like to be my age."

Memory. Not forgetting. But not insisting that what I was like at fifteen is what my daughters must be like at fifteen. It's a very different world. But the fact that I can remember my own journey into adolescence helps. The changes in the body, the readiness for new kinds of relationships, these are the same. We can talk about them and even laugh at some of the superficial differences. What has happened to white gloves? When did blue jeans become an acceptable mode of dress? When did language become acceptable on TV that would have caused a temporary blackout when I was a child? What is happening to our language? Words change. Ways of looking at people change. Sharing can become a wonderful intimacy. Sharing at deep levels, sharing grief, questions about God's love and the world's pain, having private little jokes. Remember the time we put a potato in the muffler of the car so Dad couldn't start it and didn't know we were getting him out of the house to get his surprise birthday party ready? Remember the time the puppy unwrapped all the Christmas presents while we were in church on Christmas Eve? Remember the time the oven died on Thanksgiving when we were expecting twenty people for dinner?

Remember?

All Kinds of Families

Introduction

Madeleine L'Engle

When a baby is adopted at birth, the bonding with the mother can come quickly, though the ultimate longing to find the birth mother is understandable. Sometimes it can be a wonderful experience. Sometimes it can be devastating. Sometimes it can be hilariously funny. One young woman in one of my writers' workshops wrote a series of stories about meeting her birth mother, postulating mothers of all kinds. When it actually came about, it was a letdown. Another young woman was ecstatic to discover a whole new family, with several brothers and sisters.

With Maria and me it was different because she was seven years old. We already knew each other well. We had to move from one kind of intimacy to another, much deeper one, and that took time, especially time for the little girl to find a kind of security despite her knowledge that the world is a dangerous, precarious place. That is something we all need to know, and our security comes not so much with accepting the possibility of radical change, but with the understanding that God is there, with us, at all times, no matter what happens, our only ultimate security. If we are able to understand that, then our ability to accept change and to go deeply into relationships becomes creative. Love is always trinitarian. Mother, daughter, God.

"How? How did you get me?"

"You were the one God chose for Daddy and me."

"Why?"

"Because your mommy who birthed you was very young and she wasn't able to take care of a baby, so she loved you enough to give you to another mommy who could take care of you."

"Why did you want me?"

"Because I love you. Before I ever saw you I loved you."

"How much do you love me?"

"More than tongue can tell."

"Not more?"

"The way God loves you. That's as much love as there is."

"Will you always love me that way?"

"Always."

"Even if I'm naughty?"

"Everybody's naughty sometimes."

"Will you still love me?"

"Yes. And God will, too."

Sometimes there are mothers and daughters
and no fathers.
Maybe sometimes there are fathers and daughters
and no mothers.
We come in all sorts of patterns, my mother says.
Our pattern is mother, daughter. Us two.
We are a family, she says.
Are we enough? she asks me. And then,
she answers her own question.
Yes, with God's help, we are enough.
Please be with us, God. We need you.

"I'm sorry," I said to my friend,
and that wasn't enough to say.
I put my arms around her the way
my mother had held me
and we held each other.
I didn't have any words.
What words are there when a mother dies?
"I love you," I said to my friend.
That was all.

I asked my mother, "Why?"

"Why, what?"

"Why did I get born?"

"Because your daddy and I wanted you very much."

"Me?"

"You."

"Why me?"

"Because you are the very one God chose for us, to be our very own."

"Do you still want me?"

"Always and forever."

"Does God want me, too?"

"Always and forever."

"That's good."

"It's very good. And I thank God in all my prayers."

"Okay. I guess I'll thank God, too."

My mother told me,
I didn't want to hear,
but she told me my father had left.
He would always be my father, she said,
but they wouldn't be husband and wife.
There are relationships, she said,
that just don't work out,
no matter how hard you try.
She said they really tried,
and I should try to understand.
Do I?
I knew something wasn't all right.
But do I have to understand, God?
Do I?

Dear God,
I am a daughter,
slowly moving beyond my daily needs
where I expect and accept all that is done for me.
Help me to know that one day I may be a mother, too;
not only to my own children
but to my mother,
as her needs grow greater than mine.
My mother has taught me loving and giving.
Let me never forget.

Time.
We can't stop it.
Mother, I'm grown up.
I'm ready to be a mother, too.
Like you, I will grow old.
In God's time.

My grandmother is, as she says,
becoming ancient. "It is not bad,"
she says, "and now I can say NO
to anything I want to,
and I can let people do things for me,
and I can go to bed and read silly books.
But best of all, I can see my granddaughter
growing up
into beauty and loveliness,
and I am content."